Food Zone

All About Dairy

Vic Parker

QEB Publishing

Published in the United States by
QEB Publishing, Inc.
3 Wrigley, Suite A
Irvine, CA 92618

www.qeb-publishing.com

Library of Congress Cataloging-in-Publication Data

Parker, Victoria.
  All about dairy / Vic Parker.
    p. cm. -- (QEB food zone)
  Includes index.
  ISBN 978-1-59566-769-4 (hardcover)
  1. Dairy products--Juvenile literature. 2. Cookery
(Dairy products)--Juvenile literature. I. Title.
  TX377.P365 2010
  641.3'7--dc22

                              2008056072

Printed and bound in China

Author Vic Parker
Consultant Angela Royston
Project Editor Eve Marleau
Designer Kim Hall
Illustrator Mike Byrne

Publisher Steve Evans
Creative Director Zeta Davies
Managing Editor Amanda Askew

Picture credits
(t=top, b=bottom, l=left, r=right, c=center,
fc=front cover)

Alamy Images 9b Profimedia International S.R.O, 11t
(yogurt) Sue Wilson, 11b (cottage cheese)
D. Hurst, 11b (soy products) D. Hurst, 12b Paul Carter,
13cl FAN Travelstock, 13bl Robert Morris, 13br Robert
Morris, 14cr Nigel Cattlin, 1
5t Ace Stock Ltd, 15c Bon Appetit, 18b Imagestate
Media Partners Limited – Impact Photos,
19cr Robert Harding Picture Library Ltd
Corbis 4bcr Digital Zoo, 5b Ed Kashi, 7cl Mark E
Gibson, 13t Massimo Borchi, 18tl Digital Zoo,
19bl Little Blue Wolf Productions
Photolibrary 4tr Rosenfeld, 8tr Fresh Food
Images/David Marsden, 14t Rosenfeld,
14b Fresh Food Images/David Marsden
Photoshot 12c World Pictures/Colin Matthieu,
19cl World Pictures
Rex Features 6b, Gill Allen 13cr, 14cl
Shutterstock 4tl Amieundeva, 4tc Georgy Markov,
4bl Sharon Day, 4bcl Gillian McRedel, 4br Antonio
Munoz Palomares, 5t Joao Virissimo, 6tl Sharon Day,
6tr Gillian McRedel, 6c Jean Frooms,
7t Christopher Elwell, 7cr Tan Wei Ming, 7br Henk
Bentlage, 8tl Hannamariah, 8c Gelpi, 8bl V. J.
Matthew, 8br Ingvald Kaldhussater, 9t Johanna
Goodyear, 11t (goat's milk) Jaimie Duplass,
11c Petoo, 12t Georgy Markov,13bc Jeremy Smith, 15b
Elena Schweitzer, 17 Liv Friis-Larsen,
18cl Sebastian Knight, 18cr Dmytro Korolov,
18tr Antonio Munoz Palomares,
19t AGphotographer, 19bc Lepas, 19br Eric Isselée

Words in **bold** are
explained in the glossary
on page 22.

Contents

What are dairy products?

Foods made from milk are called dairy products.

There are many different kinds of dairy products, such as yogurt, cheese, and butter. Milk can come from animals such as cows, goats, and sheep.

Yogurt

Cheese

Butter

Cow's milk

Goat's milk

4

You will need

- 4 scoops of vanilla ice cream
- 20 fl oz (600 ml) milk
- 2 tsp vanilla extract
- Blender
- Tall glasses
- Drinking straws

Make a... vanilla milkshake

1 Put all the ingredients into your blender and blend until the mixture is smooth.

2 Pour into tall glasses and drink through straws.

Milk is a liquid that contains millions of tiny drops of fat. Milk can be turned into other dairy products if it is heated, cooled, shaken, or if other ingredients are added to it.

⇨ Sometimes the drops of fat in milk float to the top, forming a separate layer. This is called cream.

5

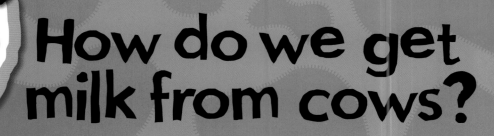

How do we get milk from cows?

Milk comes from cows that have recently given birth to young, called calves.

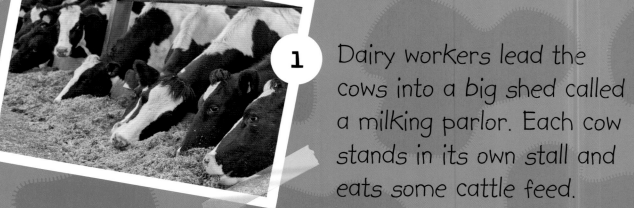

1 Dairy workers lead the cows into a big shed called a milking parlor. Each cow stands in its own stall and eats some cattle feed.

The workers attach the cows' **teats** to a milking machine. The machine takes the milk from the cows.

2

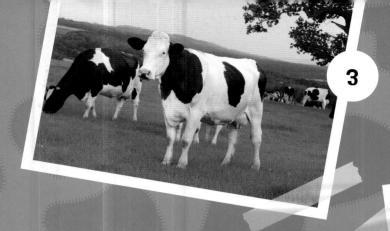

3 The cows then go back to the field.

At the dairy, the milk is separated into different parts, such as **skimmed milk** and cream.

4

5 The different parts of milk are then packaged and taken to stores.

Food news

One dairy cow produces about 33 pints (16 liters) of milk a day. That is 12,340 pints (5,840 liters) of milk in a year.

Friesian cow

7

How do we eat dairy products?

You can eat dairy products for breakfast, lunch, and dinner.

For lunch, you could eat tomato soup with a spoonful of Greek yogurt.

For dinner, you could make a baked potato with cottage cheese.

At breakfast, you might have cereal with milk.

For dessert, you could have some ice cream.

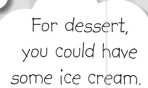

You will need

- 5 ripe bananas
- 3.5 oz (100 g) caster sugar
- 8 fl oz (250 ml) double cream
- 8 fl oz (250 ml) milk
- Blender
- Plastic container
- Bowl

Make a...
banana ice cream

1 Peel four bananas and ask an adult to blend them until they are very soft.

2 Add the milk, cream, and sugar and blend again until it is all mixed in.

3 Pour your ice cream into the plastic container and freeze it for at least six hours, until solid.

4 Serve in a bowl with your last banana.

When milk is kept in a warm place, it begins to taste **sour**. Milk products are normally kept in the refrigerator to keep them fresher for longer.

⇨ Dairy products such as yogurt and milk need to be kept in the refrigerator.

Why does your body need dairy products?

Dairy products contain many different things that your body needs.

Dairy products, such as cheese, contain **calcium**. Calcium makes your teeth and bones strong, and your nerves work properly.

Cow's milk contains vitamin B, which helps to release energy from the food you eat.

Dairy products such as yogurt have **protein** in them, which your body needs to grow.

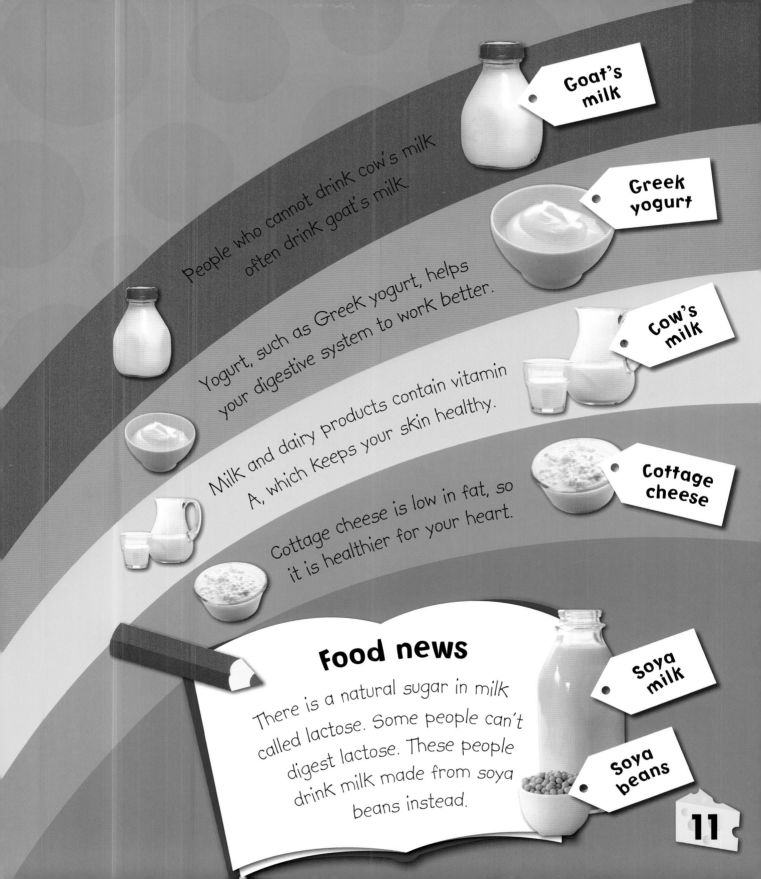

People who cannot drink cow's milk often drink goat's milk.

Goat's milk

Yogurt, such as Greek yogurt, helps your digestive system to work better.

Greek yogurt

Milk and dairy products contain vitamin A, which keeps your skin healthy.

Cow's milk

Cottage cheese is low in fat, so it is healthier for your heart.

Cottage cheese

Soya milk

Soya beans

Food news

There is a natural sugar in milk called lactose. Some people can't digest lactose. These people drink milk made from soya beans instead.

Cheese

How is cheese made?

Although there are many different types of cheese, there are four steps to making all of them.

1 **Bacteria** are added to milk, which is then heated. The milk separates into curds and whey. This is called curdling.

Next, the whey is removed. This is called draining. If a lot of whey is left, the cheese will be soft. If a lot is removed, it will be hard.

2

3 The curds can then be poured into molds to shape them.

The cheese is then left to develop its flavor. This is called ripening. Cheese can ripen for just a few hours or sometimes for several years.

4

5 The cheese is then packaged and taken to stores.

Eat a... piece of cheddar

It's the world's most popular cheese. There are more than 250 different types of cheddar.

Mild red cheddar

Welsh cheddar

White cheddar

Butter

How is butter made?

Butter is made from cream, the fattiest part of milk.

1 The cream is heated to kill any harmful bacteria in it. This is called pasteurization.

The cream is put in a churning machine. This makes the fatty part of the cream separate from the liquid part of the cream.

2

3 The fatty part of cream clumps together and becomes solid chunks of butter.

4 The butter is then packaged and sent to stores.

The leftover liquid part of the cream is called buttermilk. This can be used in baking instead of milk or cream.

5

Make a... pat of butter

1 Beat the cream in the food processor. It will gradually thicken into stiff whipped cream. When this happens, turn the speed to low.

2 A few seconds later, a chunk of yellow butter will separate from the liquid. Turn off the food processor.

3 Drain off the liquid and enjoy using your butter.

Make some yogurt cheese

It's easy and fun to make cheese using yogurt.

You will need

- 1 pt (500 ml) Greek yogurt
- Ball of string
- Long stick
- Large piece of thin, clean cloth, such as **muslin**
- Large mixing bowl
- Wholemeal bread

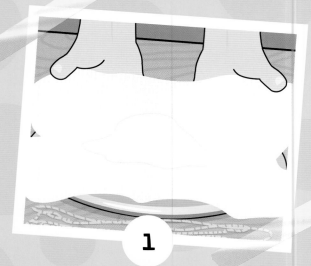

1

Put the yogurt in the middle of the thin cloth or muslin.

2 Bring the ends of the cloth together and tie it with string so the yogurt does not leak out.

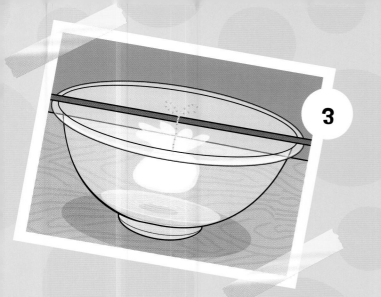

Tie the cloth to the stick so it hangs underneath. Place the stick across the mixing bowl so the yogurt hangs into it. The whey can then drain from the yogurt.

When the whey has stopped dripping from the cloth, untie the string. Make the yogurt cheese into small balls and eat it with some wholemeal toast.

Food news

Greek yogurt is usually made from sheep's milk, but can be made from cow's milk, too.

Greek yogurt

Goat's milk

Does all milk come from cows?

People use milk from many different kinds of animals.

People who live in Europe often get milk from herds of goats and sheep.

Nomads, or travelers, in hot sandy deserts keep camels for milk and transport.

In Asia and South America, people milk buffaloes.

18

Cheese can be made from different kinds of milk. Italian mozzarella cheese often comes from water buffaloes.

In Tibet and Nepal, people make a cheese called chhurpi from **yak's** milk.

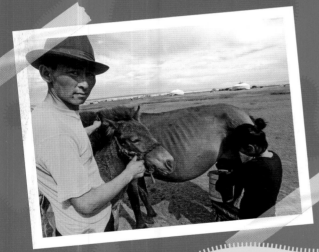

In central Asia, a yogurt drink called kefir is made from horse's milk.

Eat a... piece of Greek feta cheese

It is made from a mixture of goat's and sheep's milk.

sheep

Goat

feta cheese

Make cheesy red peppers

Try making this tasty recipe that uses cheese.

You will need

- 2 red peppers, halved
- 2 oz (50 g) long grain rice
- 4.5 oz (125 g) cheddar cheese, grated
- 1 large egg, beaten
- 1 tbsp olive oil
- 1 tsp English mustard
- 1 tbsp Worcestershire sauce
- 1 small onion, chopped
- Salt and pepper
- Baking tray
- Saucepan
- Strainer
- Mixing bowl
- Metal spoon
- Water

1 Ask an adult to put the oven on to preheat at 375°F/190°C/Gas 5.

2

Wash the rice in the strainer until the water goes cloudy. Repeat four times. Put the rice in the saucepan and cover with water.

3 Ask an adult to bring the rice to a boil. Turn the heat to low. The rice will take about ten minutes to cook.

Put the peppers on the baking tray, drizzle with olive oil, and sprinkle with salt and pepper. Ask an adult to place them in the oven for 15 minutes.

5 Mix the rice with the cheese, onion, egg, Worcestershire sauce, and mustard in a bowl.

Fill the pepper halves with the mixture. Ask an adult to put them in the oven again for 15 minutes.

21

Glossary

Bacteria
Tiny living things. Bacteria are so small they can only be seen through a microscope.

Calcium
A chemical that makes your teeth and bones hard and strong.

Muslin
A very fine cotton fabric.

Protein
Substances in some foods that your body needs to grow and repair itself.

Skimmed milk
Milk that has had the cream removed from it.

Sour
A sharp, unpleasant taste.

Teat
The part of a female animal's body that her babies suck on to drink milk.

Yak
A type of cattle with long hair and long horns.

Notes for parents and teachers

- Show the children pictures of a variety of foods and pick out which ones are dairy foods. Discuss how each dairy product is made.

- Talk about why our bodies need dairy foods to stay healthy and how much we should eat every day.

- Discuss why low-fat dairy foods are healthier choices than full-fat ones. Make a picture list of how we might choose low-fat dairy foods instead of full-fat ones. For example, choosing to have fresh fruit with yogurt instead of cream.

- Make a poster of cheeses from around the world, showing their names and what milk they are made from.

- Look for recipes for making your own yogurt. You can use a yogurt-making machine, but you do not have to—keeping the milk in a warm place will work just as well. Use full-fat milk and a few teaspoons of plain live whole milk yogurt as a starter. Add fruit and flavorings to make different kinds of yogurt.

- Talk about how we might use different types of dairy food in cooking. Make an international dairy cookbook with recipes and pictures from around the world.

Index